I0532267

Soulful Verses: Chronicles of Life, Struggle, and Redemption

Michael J. Tate

GLOBAL
PUBLISHING
SOLUTIONS

SOULFUL VERSES: CHRONICLES OF LIFE, STRUGGLE, AND REDEMPTION
by Michael J. Tate
Published by Global Publishing Solutions, LLC
923 Fieldside Drive
Matteson, Illinois 60443
www.globalpublishingsolutions.com

Library of Congress Control Number: 2024903097
International Standard Book Number: 979-8-9900270-0-8
E-book International Standard Book Number: 979-8-9900270-1-5

Printed in the United States of America

TABLE OF CONTENTS

INTRODUCTION

THE REASON I WRITE

I write for the millions of us
Who've been placed in EXILE by this society
Through past transgressions,
Honestly learning our lessons,
Making a conscious decision within our heart of hearts
To take the wisdom from these mistakes
And to use the knowledge to positively and gently guide the youth away
From this lonely path of death and self-destruction,
Because the fame and fortune
Are just too high of a price to gamble with our
Sons,
Daughters,
Mothers,
And Fathers.
Those who believed in us
Before we could fathom who we would ever be
And have left this earth before they could see us transform from boys to
men
And from girls to women.

The reason I write is for my son,
Michael Junior Tate the Second,
So that he won't have to travel through this life
Aimlessly and terrified
Of making that one mistake that might take his life away,
Because he didn't have the guidance of a loving and caring father.

The reason that I write
is because there is a difference between an explanation and justification.

This book is my explanation,
Not a shot at justifying my past actions,
So that people can understand my state of mind through these
transgressions!

PEACEFUL AND PERFECT WORLD

If this was a peaceful and perfect world,
Who would benefit the most?
Man or God?

If you have been tormented at the hands of your Father,
Mother,
Brother,
Sister, or
Friends
That make up this society,
Would you pray to your GOD to take away your torment
That you never knew existed?

If you had absolute control
Over your life,
From who were your friends,
To how much money you made,
To whom you liked,
Or even to whom you loved,
To the afflictions that infected your
Mind, body, and soul,
Which God has himself over your life,
Would you place your narcissistic pride aside
To glorify your GOD?
Who didn't even hold life or death
Over your head?

Again, I ask you
If this was a peaceful and perfect world,
Who would benefit the most?
Man or God?

NEVER JUDGE A BOOK BY ITS COVER

I am only what I want you to see,
So, before you judge me by your standards,
Come walk with me.

Because if you walk ahead of me,
I will misdirect your sense of judgment,
By continuously placing illusion in front of your face,
Because I am more than you give me credit for.

I am knowledge,
Wisdom, and
Understanding.
But you will never see these things,
Because you underestimate my intellect.

So, the next time you think of judging me
By my appearance,
You better think twice.

Because if you misjudge me,
I will defeat you every time.

TO LIVE

Sometimes in this life when all is bleak, and
All hope and loved ones have evaporated from you,
Like smoke in a gentle winter snowstorm,
and you have given up on yourself,
Your head may raise to the sky.
seeking guidance and answers.
You may also ask your GOD why has this life
robbed you of your hopes and desires.
But all you see are the soft cotton white clouds,
Drifting slowly away from you,
Only fortifying the loneliness within your heart.

There are many great truths within this world,
The most persistent one is that to live is to suffer.
No matter who you are,
You will suffer the price
For the gift of life.

In order for one to resurrect from the self-delusion of forlornness,
One must seek to find the cryptical chambers
within their heart of hearts
Because the hidden hopes and passions
Have camouflaged their essence
to the conscious mind.

Once these hopes and passions are found,
They will cradle one in their arms,
Silencing one's fears of an isolated world,
Secretly and gently guiding one back
from the abyss within their own mind.

IMAGINE ME

Imagine me
looking outside my glass window
And not seeing my people being victimized.
Whether
Native Americans,
African Americans,
Latino Americans,
Or even Europeans,
The same entity has taken that sacred oath
And sworn to protect them.

Imagine me
Being able to walk down America's streets
Without being followed,
As the lion stealthily stalks the zebra,
By my own brothers
And sister,
Because the powers that be
Have chosen to raise the price to live,
Making my people of poverty GENOCIDE ourselves
From the inside out.

Imagine me
Placing my vanity aside
To dissipate the ever-lurking CONDEMNATION
That has rooted itself within the hearts
Of my people of poverty
To uplift them into a state of stimulated consciousness.

Imagine me
Looking outside my window
Or
Walking down these American streets,
Seeing these oppressive conditions

And patiently waiting for some kind of GOD to come to save me
And my people from poverty.
Instead of loading up my Mac-90s,
AKAs,
AR-15s,
And twin fifty calibers
To declare a war on the GOD
They call the machine!

THE CHOSEN ONE

As the moon was dispersed from the night's sky,
I gave a bloodied birth to indecision.
This confusion enslaved my heart,
Awaking a savage beast that hungered for
KNOWLEDGE,
WISDOM,
and UNDERSTANDING of its environment!
Letting out a silent but piercing cry,
The beast within me began to strengthen
Until I was no longer a mortal man.
I had become a brother to a chosen circle.

Letting out another silent but piercing cry,
I began to roam the earth,
Feasting upon the minds of the knowledgeable.
The more the beast within digested wisdom,
The more powerful I became,
Changing the very essence of my soul,
Making me forsake the chosen circle of my brethren,
Because I had become higher than they could ever be.

So, no matter what path my feet stepped upon,
That path was meant to be my sitting throne,
Because I am
The Chosen One!

THE GOD

I am the God
Who will never place my chosen people into condemnation,
Because their lack of knowledge by the hands of their oppressors
Has made them transgress against me
despite my commandments
that I personally handed down to them.
Away with the corruption that this society has deemed appropriate.

I am the God
That has never walked upon water,
But will still destroy the threat to my chosen people's way of life
By those who threaten to enslave them into the false doctrine of false
Gods.
That has been stained in blood in my name.

I am the God!
A God of war,
Promising my protection to the innocent by the millions.
Declaring a spiritual war against anyone that tries to rape the minds,
Bodies, and souls
Of my chosen people.

I am the God
Of the true,
The old,
And the new,
But I mean nothing to you.
And you know this to be true!

THE MENACE

They call me the menace,
Because I believe in no God
Other than the one that lives within me
And has stripped me bare
Within my delusion of their very being.
A perfect and peaceful world.

They call me the menace.
So now I stand naked
Upon this earth with nothing to lose
and everything to gain.

They call me the menace
Because I won't follow their illusion
Of a safe and steady path.
But I create the path that's within my heart
So that I am able
To hold my fate within my hands
And mold it into what I desire it to be.
And, because they hate that I have this wisdom,
They call me the menace!

They call me the menace
Because I won't be content
With being content,
But only content
When I'm satisfied.

For these reasons,
I am the menace!

SUMMER RAIN

Cold to the touch,
Warming to my body,
Cleansing to my soul,
While filling the air,
The tears of the Gods
Flooding the earth,
Washing away
The sins of mankind.

QUESTIONS OF A FORSAKEN HEART

Where were you, God?
When I stayed up so many of those lonely and frightening nights,
Crying my soul out for some kind of comprehension of my own turmoil
and imperfections.

Where were you, God?
When I couldn't see brighter days on the horizon,
When I needed someone to walk and talk with in order to get the guilt
out of my soul.

Where were you, God?
When I needed that special someone to hold my hand,
To guide me through something called life.
When they teamed up against me,
Making me the monster that I am today.

Where were you, God?
When I needed to be taught about the perversions of the flesh,
So that I would not have fallen into the void called
Society!

BROKEN MOTHER

As she sits on her porch thinking
About her only son,
The only son she'll never get to know,
She wishes that she could travel back in time to the days of her addiction,
To choke the bottle by its neck, killing her long-time friend
Called Gin!

Wanting to see him one last time before leaving this place called Earth,
To ask for his forgiveness,
To tell him how much she has loved him,
Yet,
He is confined to a lonely cell by the sins of his so-called friends.

She knows that maybe if she had been a better mother,
He may have even been a respectable man in this life,
Maybe even changed the world!
It hurts her soul to sit and watch him struggle with himself.
All by himself.

BROKEN SON

As he sits in his lonely steel cage feeling
lost and alone,
He begins to wonder where his life went wrong.
Was it the addictions of his mother and father?
Was it that every time he tried to love someone
They seemed to push him away?
Maybe these are some of the reasons why
He cocooned himself within his hatred,
Turning his heart cold to a world that he could never comprehend.

As he sits in his lonely cell feeling scared and alone,
He begins to wonder.
Will he become another statistic?
Over something as meaningless
As his pride?
Or will he get to see the ending to his story?
But exactly what could be his ending
Other than more intense torture!

As he sits in his lonely cell feeling alone and ugly,
He begins to wonder
If anyone could ever love such an ugly soul
That has become so cold from the lies
That have become his truth.

As her son sits in his lonely cell thinking of the mother he wished he
knew,
Knowing of her hardships at the hands of her addiction within this life,
Never once would he become judgmental of his mother's actions.
Because in his heart of hearts, he knows that his mother did the best she
could for him.

AND THEY SAY PART 1

And they say that statistically
I'm not supposed to be alive today.
For the propagandists within this society
Have deemed themselves gods.
And like mice in a maze,
They have placed obstacles and resistance
At my every turn,
To analyze the pureness of my essence.
Because they are threatened by the ancient kingdom
That flows from within my heart
and through every molecule of my body
Like the Nile River through Africa,
To irrigate and stimulate the minds of the youths,
To who and what they will become
In the end
and what they were
In the beginning!

HEROES

All my heroes were turned into metallic stones!
Because their propaganda was already known
And the threat they posed to this society wasn't condoned,
Because of our cowardice they died all alone.

Forsaking and sacrificing their lives,
Families,
Hopes,
Dreams,
And Souls
To engage in a laborious imperishable embattlement
with an uncompromising nemesis,
They sat upon their golden throne
with the intent to maliciously and sadistically dictate our futures,
while condescendingly caricaturing their efforts to oppress the people.

All my heroes were turned into metallic stones!!!!!!
Their propaganda was already known,
And the threat they posed to this society wasn't condoned.
Because of our cowardice they died all alone.

DRIFT AND DIE

I'm tired of living, but yet not ready to die.
I am feeling like I'm living a phantom,
That's in search of that look in her eye
That did not stand the sands of time.

Drifting through this physical realm looking for such things as
redemption,
And other words that I can't exactly articulate at this moment in life.
But I know that when the time comes for me to comprehend those words,
I'll be ready.

But for now, I must find the answer
To why I've become so tired of this world
and the ignorant games that its people play.

I NEVER HEARD THE WARNING

Under economical jackboots,
I heard my ancestors' spirits crying out in forlornness,
But I could only at that time
Smell what I was supposed to see
And taste what I was supposed to hear.

Therefore,
I never comprehended their warning.
Instead, I chased the Gods of this society
To whom my desires worshipped faithfully.
Down a path of illuminated security,
Making me fall captive to my greatest nemesis, Myself,
To engage in a prolonged embattlement
That took me through the deepest of hell's boundaries.

MY YOUTH

I emulated my youth for knowledge.
But not common knowledge,
But the occult knowledge that man is the savage of beasts.
Ever created by the hands of God!

Because man has the knowledge of good and evil,
Even a free will,
But in times of isolation
They will turn into savage beasts.
With no emotional remorse for their actions,
Nor what damage they do to their fellow humans,
Because they only want what they desire,
And anything or anyone that interrupts this desire
Will be caught up in their rapture!

MY PAIN PART 1

He's been alone all of his life,
Running from one sin to another,
With no one strong enough to embrace his true essence.

He tried to shed his skin in order to play a role
that was never meant for him.
But being so tired of the solitude,
He was willing to try anything once to be accepted.

This solitude has blackened my heart into a state of stimulated
nothingness,
Which has numbed my heart of every emotion.
I only wish for death,
Because this world has nothing more to present to me
But what I've already seen,
A kingdom of nothingness,
My destination is a lake of fire.

But what better place for such a troubled soul
That deserves no better?
Because my past is evidence enough of
my pain.

THE FATHER

I stand here waiting
In this realm of mortality patiently and eagerly
Like a child waiting restlessly
For his mortal father to return from work,
Because I tire of the iniquities
That have rooted themselves
Within the hearts of men,
Because I've seen my share of
Death,
Disease,
Hunger,
And oppression.

Even through my wickedness,
He saw it befitting to walk me through
My trials and tribulations.
And when I stumbled to the ground,
Drowning in my own self-pity,
Wondering how much more of this life I could take,
I cried out,
Where are you, God?

Not only did he stay by my side,
But he sat to comfort me
Then picked me up to carry me
Through the flames of my depression.

THE SON

I stand here waiting in this realm of mortality,
Eagerly but sorrowful for my Christ.
Because with childlike faith
I look toward the heavens
For Him to descend from the sky
Like the mighty king He is.
But then condemnation
Descends upon my shoulders
Like a bird of prey.
Because who am I
For a King to die for?
He and only He
Knows the evilness
That my heart pumps
Through this betraying body.
But even so,
When I was swarmed
By a legion of fallen angels,
And my friends and family
Dissipated from around me,
And the demons of my yesteryears
Were determined to kill me with sin,
My Christ rose from the grave and said
Touch him not,
For he's mine!

AND THE HOLY SPIRIT

I stood on a great plateau
Overlooking the valley of death,
Of this realm of mortality.

Patiently and silently listening for the Holy Spirit,
Like a child
Intensely listening for the sound of tires treading
Upon the rocks within the driveway,
Indicating that his father
Has returned.

Because I knew that once I had the spirit of
My heavenly Father who is within me,
Who could rightfully
Stand against me?

So, you could only imagine the joy
I felt when I heard the fluttering of wings
And saw the Holy Spirit
Descending upon me
In the form of a beautiful white dove.

I knew that my heavenly Father
Had decided to build
A temple within my heart.
Spreading my wings,
I leaped from this great plateau.

Riding the currents of the wind down into the valley of the shadow of
death
To engage in spiritual embattlement,
Not once caring or thinking of my life.
Why should I care
When the living spirit of the Father

Lives within me!

IF

If you were to have everything you've ever dreamed of,
Would these things fill the emptiness
Within your life??????

If you were the king of many nations,
Would this power fill the weakness
That engulfs your mind?

If you were a holy angel
That sat at the right hand of GOD himself,
Would this pureness
Banish the evilness that flowed through your veins?

OVERCOME

As the black raven flew past my vision,
I looked into the blackened night's sky and wondered,
Will anything ever feel this good again?
But then I feel your presence
Within my soul.

So I turn to get a better look at you,
Standing tall and beautiful
Like a GOD came to Earth.
But as I got a better look,
I knew that my perception of you was wrong.
For I see you for your true nature,
You're no one other than
Satan himself.

But you won't OVERCOME me this time,
Because I know the true essence of your power.
So, if I can defeat my flesh,
Then I will defeat you.

So now we stand facing each other,
You with your beautiful smile
Of a being
That has won many of these mortal battles.
Me with my shield of knowledge,
Wisdom,
And understanding
That will win the last
And only true battle.

Screaming,
LET THE BATTLE BEGIN!

I began to charge toward you
And knew that this will be a never-ending battle,
Until my home is made in the Earth.

But I've prepared very well
For this last confrontation,
To OVERCOME the demons
That you've planted within my soul!

UNFORGIVEN

The lone Indian warrior
Stands at the top of the rocky mountain
In the heat of battle
With his silky hair
Blowing softly in the refreshing morning's air,
While reflecting on his yesteryears,
Because he knows that the moment of truth is at hand!

He's done many things within his life
That his GOD may not be pleased with.
But do these misfortunes
Make the mighty young warrior
Such a mischievous man?
Or does it only make the young warrior
Merely human?
Because his GOD
Placed him in such a betraying body
That has embraced his unforgiven ways of a society
That has made this young warrior
Fall victim to these sinful pleasures at every turn.

So now this late in his life,
Is it too much for him to ask
That he be one of
The chosen few
That will make it to the
Peaceful here and after?
Or
Should he prepare himself to die
UNFORGIVEN?

LONE WOLF

I,
The mightiest leader in the history of my pack
Made sure that they had everything that they needed.
They never hungered for food nor worried for shelter.

But the nothing in me
Stalked me after every hunt
And made me the greatest hunter ever among my pack.
Was it the same nothing within me
That made me so despised among my pack?

Because during the times of my solitude,
My detachment was their inconvenience,
Which made them turn their backs on me in disdain.
Now I find myself
A LONE WOLF.

So now I travel this snow-covered forest in search of that anything
That will unfreeze my heart!

MOTHER NATURE

You never deserved me.
Because I gave you the love,
Life,
And loyalty
That defined me as the man I am today.
But you never embraced me
For the loving son
That I've always been.

Instead
You collected all my imperfections,
Balled them up,
Then shoved them down my throat
In the attempt to break my will
And steal my dreams,
So that I would become the person
That you don't want me to be.
But my rage was too intense
For your nature
To comprehend!

LOST AND ALONE

This world has made him so violent
And emotionally tired.
Because his once held beliefs
Were proven to be illusions;
And not wanting to live in a false reality,
He had to turn his cheek
In a world that he thought he knew.

Then, at the precise moment he chose
To forsake his old life,
Confusion and loneliness
Settled upon his shoulders,
Giving way to intense anger.
With no one to run to for comfort,
He watched as his innocence slowly died.
For the ones he would've run to for comfort
Were the same ones
That taught him everything that he ever knew
To be wrong.
With nowhere to channel his anger,
It built at every thought
Of a perfect and peaceful world.

MY EYES ARE ALWAYS CLOSED

For I tire of the ignorance
Within the world.
It has camouflaged itself
Into the truth and
Manipulated millions of innocent people
Into believing
That they can do as they please
Without paying the price for their decisions.

For me to see the rich feast
Upon the forsaken and poor,
When their cups are overflowing,
It is too much for my eyes to see,
My heart to embrace,
and my mind to assimilate.

For my desires and reality
Are always in an elongated embattlement
With one another,
Which I can't seem to bifurcate.
So instead of dealing
With my imperfections,
I would rather
Close my eyes
And masquerade that
I'm without sin.

HUNDRED YEARS

Evilness is what generates the heart,
Pumping its liquefied hatred through my veins.

Motivating every thought with its faithfulness,
Overturning the righteousness of my soul,
Only clarifying the desire to deceive.
Digressing with every word spoken.

But will any of this matter a hundred years from now
When my body has left this betraying soul?

I think not!

So why not live for today,
and die for tomorrow?

ONE WITH ME

Walk with him on an expedition
To a place
Where there's nothing more than
Deception and emptiness,
Breeding an evilness
Within a boy
To the very essence
Of his being.

Fueled by the solitude
Of three lifetimes,
He tried the only way
He knew how
To silence these specters
Who rooted themselves
Within the garden
in his mind.
With no one to help him
Fight this losing battle,
These specters
Began to infest his soul;
Making me a man
I could never love
Nor be proud of.

THE DRIFTER

Lost and alone within a thick mist of pandemonium,
The drifter roams.

Dreaming of days gone by with no one or anything
to call his own.

France to England,
Africa to Paris,
Are a few of the places that he has wandered aimlessly,
Never stopping long enough to claim what's rightfully his.

On he roams.

For he has been a king among vagabonds and a vagabond among kings.
The material riches within this life have no significance to him.

On he roams.

Searching for anything
That would shadow his mind
From his transgressions of the past.

If asked what this something might be,
He would not answer you for he doesn't know himself.

On he roams.

Maybe he is still looking for that twinkle within her eye
That he lost sight of so many years ago.

Maybe he still feels the loss of
Becoming that respectable man that he's been yearning and searching for
since birth.

33

But now he will forsake such thoughts.
For they only lead him down the path
Of condemnation.

One's past is only their past.
One can't change their past
But rather use it to navigate into their sunsetting destiny;
Learning to be content with his placement in this life.

On he roams.

Slowly drifting through a thick mist of pandemonium.

For after all,
I am no other than the drifter
Who's lost and alone,
With nowhere to call my home!

IGNORANCE

As ignorance descends upon my shoulder
Like a spectral hand,
I slowly lower my head
And say a silent prayer,
To the Virgin Mary
For my soul.
Because it's only known to me
That the never dying
Remains of ignorance
Will be the death of me.
Forever using its gift
With words,
To cloud the mind and hearts
Of millions,
So that it will turn its lies
Into my life.

A LIGHT THROUGH THE NIGHT

This world is so dark
That I've become afraid
That I may stumble
Over my own instincts.

And at the end of this bone-shattering fall,
I'm afraid
That I may break my confidence
And the foothold that I have in this life.

My desires make me no different than the rat
That risks his life for a piece of cheese,
For I constantly risk my life
Over a small piece of meaningless act.

Hopefully,
Before I take this trip
I can find
A light through the night.

PATIENTLY WAITING

For twenty-eight years I've hidden
Within the shadows of the blades of grass,
Patiently waiting
For someone
Or
That something to light my fuse
So that I could explode into flames
and rise above Mother Earth,
Because I've become
Emotionally and mentally tired
Of the embryonic and economic games
That people and the government play
And of the ignorance that lies awake
Within their thought processes.

For twenty-eight years
I've danced on the very edge
Of my sanity,
Patiently waiting for her face
That will set my mind at ease,
Like an October Sunday morning
Or
That transcendent smile that makes me feel as if I've just landed on the
sun.
But just maybe
This is my sentence after the trial,
To remind me
Of all the women
That I've transgressed against
In my days of incompetent youth.
So I won't complain too much,
But rather keep my faith and keep
Patiently waiting.

THE UNKNOWN

There are secrets within his mind
That he's afraid to face on his own.
So he gives himself illusions
To face another day.
Because to face the truth
Would make him ashamed of the person
That he sees in the mirror.
So he continues to digest lies,
Because he's too frightened
To face the unknown
and change his sinful ways.

You might see me as a coward,
and rightfully so, I would agree.
But before you do such a thing
You must understand my homeland.
For we take pride in and love the things
Where no such man should rightfully love
Or have pride for.

But this is my homeland.
The only one I've ever known.
To choose another
Would lead to walking blindly.

BLEEDING HEART

My heart bleeds for the simplest of minds,
For they honestly don't know what they have done.
They spend their whole life
In a sea of confusion,
Running from one leader
To another.
Never once stopping to think for themselves.
Constantly being controlled
By the powers that be.
Never taking the time to search their hearts
To find out what they want
From this life
Or themselves.

My heart bleeds for the broken-hearted,
Because they have sworn to never love again.
They run from the love that they find from others for themselves.
They are too afraid to embrace dreams of hope,
Ignorant to the fact of true love.
Settling for abstract love, they are too afraid to go without love.
But more frightened to love someone,
They let their lives enclose around another's
Bleeding heart.

REDEMPTION

Redemption is a ten-letter word
That most people spend their lives trying to obtain.
But most people won't comprehend its seriousness,
And even fewer
Will be able to grasp its memory.

We have only one lifetime
To obtain this understanding,
But even less time to find it
On this short journey called life.

But once everyone can comprehend
That redemption can only be obtained
At the foot of the creator,
Their journey will come full circle,
and they will finally find peace
Within their mind,
Body,
And soul!

WASTED TIME

As I sit here
In a void of compassion,
Chained to my nature,
I look out the window
To see a beautiful spring day.
I've taken them for granted
For so many years.
But now that it is forbidden to me
I start to think about
Everything that I've missed.

The look of love within her eye.
The slap on the back
By a proud brother.
The dying of a beloved uncle.
A gentle hug from a mother.
The looks of gratitude from a younger brother,
And looking at the setting of a November sun
With a wife
That I will never know,
All these things I've missed.
For I've chased illusions
Of self-worth
While drowning in a sea
Of low self-esteem.

As I return
From this mental expedition,
I notice that the night sky has silently crept up
Outside my window,
and I begin to realize

That I've wasted more time

Trying to justify
My lack of responsibility
To you.

But why should I care?
I'm having too much fun
Hiding behind you,
For I've only wasted my life.

MY LAUGHTER

Just because you hear my laughter,
Don't fall for the illusion
That I'm a happy man.
For my laughter is only symbolic
Of the never-ending hatred
That has begun to consume
My heart.
So, the next time
You hear my laughter
Be afraid.
Be very afraid.

They say that time heals everything.
But I must disagree.
For my hatred
Is my Alpha and Omega.
It was the birth of me
And it will be
The death of me.
For time only soothes
My hatred
For small periods of time,
But never heals it.

Therefore,
The next time you hear
My laughter
Be afraid.
Be very afraid.

For my laughter
Is only symbolic
Of my never-ending hatred.

BAGGED LADY

As she sits on the park bench humming to herself,
Watching as the people pass her by,
Not one once gives her a passing glance.
They look down upon her with contempt
As she asks them with shame in her eyes,

"What little may you spare?"

They only ignore her.
They never take the time to know of her hardships;
Or just to befriend her just for the moment.
Never realizing how fast life could turn on them
And how easily they could become a bag lady themselves!

CHANGE

Change and time are the essence of humanity,
Because nothing that pertains to change comes without time.

So forgive me
While I stumble over my past transgressions
and with forbidden fruit,
which seems to lurk in the shadows
Of my everyday life.

Like an unnatural being that's been patiently waiting
To devour the righteousness of my soul,
Leaving me alone
To struggle endlessly with my vanity.

But
On the horizon,
Like a newly born December morning,
I see change for my life, and granted the time,
Change will persist!

YOU CAN LET GO NOW

I have been addicted
To the way the sun
Has risen at my every command
and the mightiness of my kingdom.
This addiction has made me feel
Like I'm more than I really am,
To the point of conceit.
But somewhere deep within my soul
I hear a voice telling me,
"YOU CAN LET GO NOW."

The illusion and the deceit
That I've cast upon this land
Have become my bitter-tasting truths.
Uprooted the utmost respect
That I demand from one and all
Who have the courage to enter into my presence.
But as they tell me their requests,
I hear a voice within my mind
Telling me,
"YOU CAN LET GO NOW."

As an old and graying king
That's about to be dethroned,
I try to remember all the nations
That I brought to their knees,
and not one comes to mind.

But I do remember all of my regrets of the past 28 years
Which seem to play themselves out
Within my mind's eye.

Upon this throne,

I ask myself,
Was all that pride and search for self-worth
All in vain?
Then I begin to comprehend
What I've been trying to tell myself
Over and over again.
At that moment of clarity
I decided to let my pride drift into nothing,
Like a car into a spring morning's fog.
Then I close my eyes,
Because I've made my peace with the Creator,
So I finally let go to gain eternal life!!!!!!

MY BROTHER

As I lie here in this darkened wasteland
I scream,
BROTHER!
Why have you forsaken me
To fight my fears all alone?
You are so intent on stripping me of my pride
That you never foresaw
That I'm here to catch you
If you were to ever fall.

Can't you see
That if we were to put our minds together
No one could move against us?
But you would rather rape my mind
Instead of encouraging me.

So here I lie by the gutter
Crying for you, brother,
For your soul filled with corruption.

Hopefully,
One day someone will come along
To help you cleanse your soul.
But until that day
I will lie here and pray for you.
That you'll see that the path you're taking
Will only lead you to your destruction.

So here I lie
Seeking no vengeance,
'Cause no matter how you have treated me,
You're still my BROTHER!!!!!!

DEATH AND DESTRUCTION

He's never known unconditional love,
Nor eternal happiness.
He's only held hands
With his hatred and solitude.

Until now he was certain
With his place in this life.
So why now must he wish
To be loved and understood;
And his heart yearns
To love another?

He's never seen the sunlight
That would light his way
Into true love.
For the darkness and rain
That have engulfed his preparation
Make it hard for him
To get a footing on his life.
So he continues
To struggle over obstacles
Of his unconscious making.

Where is the GOD of Abraham
That helped Moses part the Red Sea?
Maybe He's forsaken
One of his mortal children.
Or maybe I was cursed
From birth.

So I will continue
To step down the path
Of death and destruction,

Never wishing to seek happiness.
For to do so
I would be only deceiving myself.

HOPE THROUGH THE DAY

It seems like every second of the day
I'm intensely grasping for anything
That will lead me
Through the colorless body of my thoughts,
In order for me to keep my dreams alive
When I'm in a society
That seems to want to take them away
So they can feed my imperfections
To the soulless and hopeless.

But I've been down
This road before.
On second thought
It's been the only road
I've ever known.
But these obstacles and resistance
That life seems determined
To place before me
Won't make me turn and run,
Because I'm not made like that.

So now that I'm here
and see that everything around me is gone,
I begin to comprehend
That there's nothing to be afraid of.
And with this wisdom
I gain security and confidence
That this life
Won't break me down,
Because I'm already broken and bloodied.

IN EXILE

Waiting for the day
When I can feel the warmth
Of the sun against my face
and smell the freshness
Of a newly grown daisy.

I know that this day will come.
But until then I must pray
That I can move it out of my mind,
Body, and soul.
For I know how delicate
My essence is at the moment,
and one false move or step
Will be the equivalent
Of flushing my life down the toilet.

I know the rules
and have played this game for many years,
and to forfeit now
Would be to sit back
and wait for my death.
Even though I hate this game
With every ounce of my body,
I must play
Or
Pay the consequences
Of losing more
Than I'm willing to give.
Therefore,
I will continue to play
Until I'm out of exile.

SELF-MADE PRISON PART 1

They would rather roam free
As the wild buffalo
and take their chances of dying
In the sights of the hunter's rifle,
Than to live in today's society.
Where one man's words will delete their futures,
And where they must play by another man's rules
In order to gain proper respect.

They would rather fly free
As the blackened raven
And take their chances of dying
At the end of the child's slingshot
Than to live in today's society
Where one must build a fortress
To enclose their hearts
From the wicked games these people play.

But somewhere in the process
Of building their protective fortress
They never thought
To place windows or doors,
To let themselves escape
When the time was right,
Making their protective fortress
Into a self-made prison.

I would rather die
A bloodied death
From the hunter's rifle,
Than to be entrapped
Within my self-made prison.

TO CHASE NOTHING

For they want
What they could never grasp,
And they want
What they can't see.
But to chase nothing
Is the only thing to chase.
For to chase anything worldly
Is too easily obtained.
But if they forever chase nothing,
Then they will always have goals.

MY RAGE

Trying to see through the inner rage;
To use the negative energy in a sensible way.
But they can't see the evilness that controls his soul,
Nor
Can they see through the illusion of kindness.

So why can't these people hear reason?
Why must I use my rage to break through their defenses?
Only my rage is heard
and my kindness is only a whisper upon deaf ears.

But it must be heard.
It's the only way that my soul can be at peace.
So I will conjure my inner rage to get these people to open their eyes,
For any other kind of emotion is always taken as a weakness.

I will destroy any and everyone who refuses to hear me out,
To let them see that there's no ending to the strength of my rage,
And only when I'm heard will I return to my spiritual nature.

DOWN FOR THE COUNT

They thought that I was down for the count,
But I was only taking a breather
To bring my never-ending hatred
Upon this society
That has tried to redirect my perception of the truth.
But now that they have me within their grasp,
They have finally realized that my hatred is a force
To reckon with.
It has no ending
and refuses to be contained.
For it has been bottled up too long
To accept "no" from this life.

They thought I was down for the count
and were overjoyed at the thought of my failing,
But I was only taking the time to channel my inner hatred,
and now that I have regained my footing,
I will continue to be a street disciple for the struggle.
Going to war with every and anyone that tries to control the minds of my
people prejudicially.

They thought I was down for the count,
But I was only lying in the shadows,
Watching and waiting
To grab my life by its neck,
So that I could drain the past mistakes from my veins.

A LETTER TO THE MOTHERLAND PART 1

They raided our underground libraries
and stole hundreds of years of knowledge
That our ancestors had gathered for us.
Seized my tribe from the beauty of our Native Land,
Where lions and zebras roamed the land together in harmony.

Packed in their ships as if we were nothing but cattle headed to the
market for slaughtering.
Brought to this Godforsaken no-man's-land.
They raped my beautiful tribal queen for her exotic looks
and hated me for the color of my skin.
Forbidden to speak in my native tongue,
Placed irons around my ankles and wrists,
Gave me a new name,
Watched as I plowed their fields.
My queen picked their cotton from early morning until well into the
coming of darkness.
Beaten when we didn't move with the quickness that their demands
required.
They called my tribe "lazy people."